I'm Not Really Fifty

GW00706148

Jean Dawn Leigh

jadie BOOKS

Published by
Jadie Books 2005

Copyright © Jake Adie
2005

ISBN 0 9527082 7 2

Illustrations by Ian West

Typesetting by Jake Adie

Printed & bound by
Northstar Design
Colne
Lancs
BB8 9DB

Me Fifty?

Now, there are just a few days to go and I really must control myself. Must calm down and think this thing through. Now, let me see if I can get my head around this once and for all. Nice and slow. Right, I'm a woman in her late forties who's already had a considerable number of birthdays. All right, forty-nine.

And I've another one approaching shortly. Forty-nine add one equals . . . No, it's impossible. That's what I keep coming up with and it simply cannot be true. FIFTY? Ugh, it sounds dreadful, absolutely dreadful. Must pull myself together — it isn't really happening — I must have made a mistake. I never was any good with sums. Sooner or later it will be obvious and I'll stand back and laugh at this whole ghastly business. You see, I *know* I'm not about to be fifty even though the signs suggest otherwise. I'm fully aware of what constitutes an FYO and I don't mind telling you it doesn't resemble me in the slightest. Not even close. FYOs have a sort of inbuilt seniority about them, don't they? A kind of innate maturity that enables one to recognize them from great distances. I've been aware of them for years. In fact, I can even remember one or two of my schoolteachers who were FYOs. Their kind were simply everywhere. I wouldn't be at all surprised if many of them were well into their sixties or seventies these days. It's quite absurd to expect me to be joining their ranks within a matter of days.

You have only to listen to an FYO speak to tell the difference. You must have heard them. They seem to automatically exude an air of authority that just wouldn't seem right for a younger person like me. I mean, I've not been around nearly long enough to carry it off. No one would believe me. I'd come across all kind of, er, well, sort of, ehm, well, young, immature. I just wouldn't be convincing. So, whatever happens by way of birthdays, nothing's going to suddenly transform me into the sort of person who is fifty. It just wouldn't work. Right that's that sorted out but what am I to do about the actual day? People will want to give me greetings cards with great big fives and zeros on them. How can I stop that? Well, I can't, obviously. They'll just have to labour under the misapprehension that I'm something I know full well I'm not. But should I tell them? Confront them in a sympathetic way so as not to embarrass them? Might be an idea. But would they believe me? Wouldn't the mathematics look just a little strange to them as well? They might go away thinking I'm a bit soft in the head. Talk about me behind my back. I couldn't bear that, really. But then, what choice do I have? Either I go headlong into the whole affair and attempt to redefine the very image of FYOs or I hold my head up high, irrespective of others' opinions, and approach the event with the magnanimity it deserves. Ehm, I think that's what I'll do, ignore everyone else and continue as the sub-FYO I know I am.

Of course, the more intelligent acquaintances I have will understand the situation without my needing to bring it to their notice. For a start, they'll be only too aware of the differences in our choices of . . .

Clothes

But what will the others expect me to wear? Really, this whole business is becoming silly. Me dressing like an FYO? What will they think of next? Honestly. I suppose as soon as the big day is over I'll be expected to pop down to the high street and kit myself out with a whole new wardrobe. Well how else could I pull off a

convincing impersonation of an FYO? I certainly couldn't attempt it in the rather trendy outfits I wear at the moment. You know, even though I say it myself, a woman only half my age would be proud to pick any item at random from the collection I have accumulated over the years. And now, for the sake of tradition,

I am required to donate the lot to a jumble sale so as to make room for my new fuddy-duddy image. Well, I can tell you now, there is no way I intend to do any such thing. I'm jolly well going to continue behaving like the youthful forty-something that I am. I'm just not cut out to be an FYO and that's all there is to it. I mean, if I give in so easily on this one, in a few years' time I'll be expected to join the ranks of the sixty-year-olds. And they're pensioners for goodness sake. It's outrageous. Asking a woman of my age to throw in the towel at a moment's notice when I've spent my whole life nurturing the not inconsiderable feminine attributes that

the Good Lord
bestowed upon
me. No, it just
isn't on. This is
one time when I
have no
alternative but
to put my foot
down. The
condition will
neither suit me
nor appeal to me
and, for once in
my life, I intend
to carry on doing
things *my* way.
This is not a
personal thing
you understand.
I know a good
many FYOs who

are perfectly nice people and I have no desire to openly criticize their sartorial judgement. But they are, after all, dyed-in-the-wool FYOs and would look rather ridiculous dressed any other way. Those frumpy, tweedy, two-pieces look fine on them, really, and I have no wish to be offensive. But they're hardly going to turn heads now, are they? Let's be honest with ourselves. What kind of male is going to stretch his neck to get a second look at what's inside an outfit like that? I mean, come on girls, let's be serious about this.

As far as clothes are concerned, I wish to make one thing absolutely clear: my wardrobe will remain precisely as it is for a very long time to come and, like it or not, those who have seen fit to make the quite unnecessary transition from forty-something to FYOdom will just have to put up with the sight of me carrying on as I always have. And if that's a problem, it certainly isn't mine. There, got that off my chest. Now, if you're not already convinced, let me give you an example of why I am not an FYO. Take a listen to their kind of . . .

No, all right, you don't actually have to listen to it; just contemplating it will be sufficient. Now, I wouldn't go as far as to describe myself as a purist, more of an enthusiast really. What I mean is, I've no hard and fast rules on what is good and what is bad but I know when I like something. And when that happens there is

simply no stopping me. Especially when I'm in the house on my own. That's when the hi-fi really gets a chance to prove what it's made of. Just as well, I suppose, with my voice. However, I've always tended to keep up with the latest releases and I can't imagine ever wanting things to be any different. What would Thursday night be, I ask you, without TOTP? It is Thursday, isn't it? No? Well when is it then? So, it will come as no surprise to you to learn that the prospect, all of a sudden, of having to leap up and down at a James Last concert, quite literally, fills me with horror. And if it's not Mr. Last and his band of merry codgers it'll be some embarrassing, religious, gospel, happy-clappy extravaganza at church. What a simply dreadful thought. But have you ever stopped to consider the common thread that runs through these ghastly events, eh? No? Well let me bring you up to speed. (Up to speed! — you won't hear an

FYO using trendy terminology like that every day of the week.) The ingredient essential for mass FYO hysteria is mock-youthfulness. Think about it. What is it that the respective audiences are encouraged to engage in the moment the first note is struck? That's right, movement. I say *movement* rather than *dancing* because it is generally recognized that anything more strenuous than a steady sway from side to side with the hands clapping roughly in time with the beat would, God forbid, be tempting fate. No, dancing is definitely out. Good Lord, you'd have to forget all about an encore; it'd be more a case of a mass outbreak of exhaustion before the end of the first number if they encouraged proper dancing. No, the whole point of the semi-physical fervour that these acts are given licence to promote is that the audience actually go away thinking they are still young. Deluded into believing they are still able to bop all night when all they've actually done is quivered for a couple of hours on the spot. Of course, *we* know there's a difference but that's no reason why we should spoil it for them. They go home happy, Mr. Last sells a few more albums and the overflowing collection plates keep the minister in groceries for another week.

Everyone's wins. But that doesn't mean they stand a chance in hell (if you'll excuse my language) of recruiting yours truly. Oh no, don't you even think about it. I'm quite happy with my sixties nights at the Palais thank you very much. I've years to go before I turn into an FYO.

You see, when you look at it like this, it is rather

difficult not to avoid becoming one, don't you think? And it certainly doesn't stop there. Can you imagine how they fair with . . .

I'll have to be careful with this one because I really have no desire to appear unsympathetic towards those caught in the rather ugly trap that tends to ensnare women the moment they cross the FYO threshold. Fortunately, no such entrapment will succeed in luring me but that's really not the point, is it? My heart goes

out to those poor souls whose other halves suddenly find themselves suffering under the curious delusion that younger females might prefer their company to that of *their* contemporaries. The young ladies, of course, feel no such inclination but this, sadly, has no effect on the optimism of the poor, ill-informed male. He will refuse to hear one word said against the idea particularly if voiced, with the very best of intentions, by his good lady. No, the cerebral matter hitherto dedicated to the act of reasoning rapidly hands over all future judgmental responsibility to an alternative anatomical item not famed for its ability to think straight. But he knows best and there is no stopping him. So, where does this leave our redundant FYO? Is she finished or does she, too, have fresh opportunities queuing on the horizon? Well, no, not really. But, unlike me, she did rather volunteer for this FYO lark in the first place. Not really on to start blaming someone

else, is it? Should
have seen it
coming.
However, there's
no mileage in
dwelling on it so
we must consider
her options.
Well, there are a
variety of
organizations
formed for the
express purpose
of providing
comfort for
obsolete
members of
society so she
could consider
the merits of
sitting in a circle

with like-oriented souls every Wednesday morning to bore herself silly with their problems. Or she could give herself a good shake and decide to do something more positive. Something to fill the void left by her recalcitrant partner. Something to cheer her, to introduce a little lost humour into her life. And what better way than to call up an old girlfriend and innocently pop into the pub he's decided to frequent with his new found plaything? If that won't be a bundle of laughs nothing will. With the two of them poised at a nearby table, the spectacle of him fumbling over his words, tripping over the chair leg and using every muscle he can lay his hands on in a vain effort to reduce his waist measurement to something resembling that of a man thirty years his junior will, believe me, be worth every second of his absence. In fact, on the strength of such an opportunity, I'm rather tempted to apply for full FYO membership myself. But, of course, it isn't just my decision and I'm only too aware of the sheer magnitude of my other half's feelings towards me. No, it's simply not an option in my case. You know something, he's so incredibly considerate that just recently he's enrolled me for a series of weekends away at one of the country's top health and fitness farms. He really is such a dear. The cost to him must have been immense and, in addition, he'll have to see to all his own chores while I'm away. Now that's what I call a sacrifice. Pure selflessness. But then, I suppose he realizes I'm rather special and is, presumably, prepared to keep things that way regardless of his own expense and discomfort. How

lucky am I? You know, in years to come I'll probably look back on my successful avoidance of FYOdom as the best decision I ever made.
But the plight of our FYOs doesn't stop there, think of what they have to do to their . . .

Hairstyles

Well they would, wouldn't they? I mean, they'd look totally ridiculous attempting, against such insurmountable odds, to appear like sub-FYOs. It just wouldn't work. No chance. For a start, a youthful hairstyle like mine would look absurd with all those frumpy clothes they wear. It'd draw too much attention to

them. The wrong sort of attention. You know, sniggers, that kind of thing. Life would become so em------barrassing that they'd end up being terrified to be seen in public. Luckily, of course, the vast majority of FYOs need not concern themselves on this front as nature invariably obliges by passing the required message to each remaining follicle to ensure that carefully selected strands of all future growth emerge with a positive grey tint. So, in most cases, the transformation is automatic. Everything is kind of done for them. Not a bad facility when you think about it, eh? But what confuses me is, they can't all, simultaneously, undergo the necessary conversion overnight, surely. Nature doesn't work that way. So, how come they all look the same? Peculiar or what? Well, I've got a theory. I reckon those less fortunate souls who don't find themselves quite so well served have no choice but to confront the stylist at the local salon in an effort to have the stubborn locks suitably de-coloured. Not all of them of course. No, no, no, there's more to it than that. *They* should be so lucky. No, the skilled hairdresser has, no doubt, been especially trained to remove varying amounts of natural colour from strand to strand so as to give the effect that the hair has undergone the process unassisted. Not an easy exercise I should imagine but I can't think of any other logical explanation. FYOs have to look natural after all.

But it can't stop there. No, it must get even more complicated. There are inevitably extreme cases where FYOs find themselves in the distressing position of suffering from no follicular degeneration whatsoever. None. Full head of original colour — no different to a woman thirty-years younger. Can you imagine? Some people are just born unlucky. So, for these poor individuals, there must be no option other than to have their entire mop, firstly, dyed with a plain grey tint before undergoing any number of highlighting applications to accurately match the various grey hues present in the real thing. Only then will our FYO feel she has the self-assurance to step out into the street with her head held high confident in the knowledge that *she* meets the required FYO identification criteria. In these politically correct times, you will appreciate, it is essential that one should take every care to see that one's appearance conforms properly with one's chronological development. There's probably a European statute governing it, for

God's sake.
But thank
goodness I have
no such worries.
I dread to think
what it must be
like to arrive at
such an un-
friendly juncture
with no means of
escape. No, I
have neither the
desire nor the
intention to even
consider
becoming an
FYO. They're
welcome to it.
Which brings me
to another thing
. . .

Holidays

Have you ever considered the FYO attitude towards holidays? Have you? Of course you have. We've all heard the stories as well, haven't we? All been bored rigid by them. And the photographs. What is it with women once they reach the age of fifty? Is it that much of a raw deal not to be young any more? Is it? Well it

obviously is because we all have to endure the interminable lead up to where they're going, why they're going and with whom they're going for weeks and weeks before the event. And then we're all granted a brief two-week respite for the duration of their break (unless, of course, we are unfortunate enough to actually go with them) before spending a similar, subsequent period, listening to the grisly details. No, that's unkind — but anyone would think they were the only ones who went away. I mean, we all go, don't we? Always have done. But I suppose that's it really. They're so convinced that us youngsters have a wonderful time that they're petrified of the thought of missing out on something. What else could it be? What else would cause them to think we can't wait to know the name of the wine waiter at the hotel they return to each year? Who cares? They speak as though the poor chap is resigned to fifty-weeks of sheer hell for being deprived of their company and can hardly control his enthusiasm the moment they enter the restaurant. And, of course, in reality he can't remember them from Adam. He only knows their names because he has access to the bloody hotel register. He's just being professional, for goodness sake. But he simply adores their new outfits! Like heck he does!

And that's another thing: outfits. Or, rather, the lack of them. What possesses a newly-enrolled FYO to suddenly decide that the world is ready for them to reveal, in public, what they have hitherto chosen to hide to all and sundry since the onset of puberty? What makes

them think
anyone is
interested?
Because if it's
not an audience
they're after then
what, I ask you,
is it? And why
have they left it
so long? Wouldn't
it have been far
more discreet to
have been
indiscreet at an
earlier age?
Time, after all,
does rather
delight in
charging us
dearly for the
pleasures of

longevity. Nothing comes for free. And from my experience, it seems that boobs attract a higher premium than most anatomical appendages. So much so that, as the years advance, the general desirability of their size tends to be inversely proportional to the opposite sex's wish to ogle at them. So what is

the point in 'baring all' at the precise moment nature decides it's time to pay up? Wouldn't it be more appropriate for such demands to coincide with a general trend to cover everything up? Or is it a last-ditch attempt to turn otherwise disinterested heads? Who knows?
I am just grateful that I've

managed to avoid the whole damn charade. But then the whys and wherefores of parading topless on the beach have been of little concern to me and my partner since our recent conversion to the delights of naturist holidays. Which, you will be quick to agree, bear no relation whatsoever to the above, somewhat vulgar practice. No, we choose to behave strictly as God had intended so, of course, any unhealthily inclined thoughts couldn't be further from our minds.

You see, whichever way you look at it, I'm simply not cut out to be an FYO. I don't even like their. . .

Well, would you? All right, we're all aware of the problems with food. Yes, you've got it; it has a tendency to be made with those horrible little calorie things that taste simply divine. Agree? Of course you do. And I've no desire to single out the poor, unfortunate FYO in this respect because, if I'm absolutely honest, we girls

all feel exactly the same about them. Don't we just loathe their very existence? We even despise the word itself, don't we? I mean, just take a look at it: CAL-OR-IE. The three most detestable syllables in the English language. Whose idea was it to arrange seven quite innocuous letters into such a ghastly order? Surely, any other word would have done. There must be countless other unused permutations that would have dealt with the subject far more subtly. The word just seems to delight in shouting at you if you so much as glance in the general direction of the fridge. The government organization responsible for the necessary labelling legislation may just as well oblige manufacturers to print, 'HA, HA, HA, WOULDN'T YOU JUST LOVE TO SINK YOUR TEETH INTO WHAT'S INSIDE THIS BOX? WELL, YOU CAN'T BECAUSE IT'LL MAKE YOU FAT AND NOBODY WILL WANT TO BE YOUR FRIEND' on the packaging in bold capitals.

Difficult to know why the retailers put up with it, after all, it can hardly assist in increasing sales. But, to return to our FYOs, there's another thing I can't fathom out. Just as confusing in a way. I know we all understand the reason for our vigilance where pound-accumulating foodstuffs are concerned. There's no mystery at all; men simply find leaner women more attractive. Straightforward enough? Of course it is. That's why we're all gathered together on this planet of ours. To lure gorgeous hunks and make babies with them, right? And if it's skinny females that gorgeous hunks like making babies with then skinny females it has to be. Not our fault, it's the hunks'. If they suddenly started setting their baby-making sights on big, fat, roly-poly mamas, we'd all rush down to the foodstore and buy up every calorie we could lay our hands on. And we'd probably grow to like the word as well. Well, maybe that is taking things a touch too far.

Anyway, my point is, if you haven't guessed it already, why do post-menopausal FYOs continue to behave as if they still want to make babies? Hasn't anyone told them? Or have I been saddled with the job of delivering the message via these pages? Surely not. It's preposterous to expect me to do society's dirty

work just
because I've
decided to print a
few home truths.
I didn't have to
write this book. I
could have done
something else
and then what
would we have
done? Ehm? Can
you answer that?
No, I thought
not. No different
to all the rest. If
a problem has to
be faced, leave it
for someone else.
Typical British
lethargic be-
haviour.

Well, I'm afraid I'm going to have to disappoint you. You go and do your own dirty work and leave me to get on with my book. Why should I be expected to break the news to our FYOs that they're wasting their time? All that calorie-counting and weight-watching — completely unnecessary, the lot of it. If I ever fall foul of this

FYO business I'll jolly well stuff myself silly with chocolate cakes. Loads of them. The fattier the better. And lots of fresh cream and biscuits and toffees and jam sandwiches and crisps and, well you name it, I'll stuff it. Perhaps it wouldn't be so bad after all. No, I mustn't get things out of perspective, there's more to being an FYO than merely gorging oneself. There's the little matter of their

. . .

Now you mustn't misunderstand me when it comes to the delicate matter of FYOs and their friends. There is, of course, nothing intrinsically wrong with them. As far as I can be certain, they started out in life like any other rational individual. Just like you and me. Quite normal. But then strange things happen

when you reach your half-century. Life seems somehow to overtake you in a similar fashion to what happens to those not-so-good, long-distance runners who, towards the latter stages of a gruelling race, find that the leading athletes are, somewhat curiously, approaching them from behind rather than disappearing further into the distance ahead. And, of course, they are inevitably made to look somewhat redundant by getting in the way of those still competing in the event. It might be a little cruel for me to suggest it, but why don't they just step to one side, don their track suits and head off in the general direction of the changing rooms? I know what you're thinking, if it was my son or daughter I'd be livid with anyone having the audacity to make such a suggestion. Well, I suppose you're right. But what I'm really getting at is, after FYOs spend what appears to be an incredibly short period of time accustoming themselves to the idea of being parents, one day, right out of the blue, their own kiddies announce that *they're* about to become parents. About to have *their* own kiddies. And like the athlete, the event tends to throw the mind into a state of acute turmoil. Well it would, wouldn't it? There you are going about the business of bringing up a family of little tots when, all of sudden, one of them starts to take over your role. And at their age! It really isn't on, is it? I mean, when FYOs began *their* families they were adults so it is understandable that the prospect of a mere child attempting to emulate the process will present itself as something of a shock.

But here's the real rub. Not being content with robbing you of your newly-found role as a responsible and caring parent, the youngster then decides to strip you of your office and relegate you to the status of, wait for it: grandparent. I'm not kidding. They really do that to you. Although it's no immediate consolation, the fact that the selfsame thing is likely to occur to them just a few years later does tend to lend a certain light-heartedness to the situation. However, the real purpose for my bringing this strange phenomenon to your attention is to muse over the fact that the sum total of an FYO's circle of friends quickly becomes limited to, you've guessed it: grandmothers. Just imagine. Without prior warning, all of your girlfriends are perched on rocking chairs in front of an open fire with a shawl draped around their shoulders. Can you imagine anything more depressing? One minute you're dropping the kids off at play-school and the next you're

fumbling about at the onset of senility.
It really does happen — I've actually seen it. It's another one of those numerical conundrums where the sums sort of play tricks with you. You know the length of time it takes to get from being a toddler to an adult? Yes? One's childhood. Lasts forever, doesn't it? Well, why

doesn't it take anything like as long for one's own children to go through the same process? See. Same problem. No answer to it. Beyond the realms of science. Just happens.

So, you can imagine how delighted I am to be avoiding FYOdom. The way I see it is, if I refuse to make the transition,

then my kiddies
will be
snookered.
Totally impotent.
Powerless. I get
to remain a
forty-something
and the kids can
do nothing about
it. Clever or
what? And in the
process I won't
have to bother
myself with
FYO-style

. . .

This, I am afraid, is where FYOs come into their own. Gone are the days when they need to supplement the family income by maintaining their own career. One breadwinner is more than enough to keep the wolves from the door providing, of course, one's wealth-generating partner has successfully

survived the dolly-bird phase intact. The nest has been well and truly vacated by all successfully-reared offspring leaving mother hen's rich abundance of parental skills totally obsolete. Honed to perfection over the years but suddenly of no use whatsoever. Waste bin fodder. That's all. Surplus to requirements. And to make matters worse, they're of no use to anyone else. None at all. In the intervening years, without notice, the goal-posts have been re-sited and the rule books rewritten. May as well be in a different language. All of the hard-earned experiences gathered along the way have nothing but salvage value. If they could be bound up and boxed you'd donate them to the nearest charity shop. That's what they're worth. Nothing. So, one has no choice but to return to 'Go', start over and grab some new hobbies to pass away the remaining time. Now if you think life appears to be getting a little dull do not despair. Things are about to improve beyond all recognition. You see, while it's true that you have arrived at one of life's metaphorical crossroads, there are exciting times ahead. No need to worry about redundant skills after all. No, there's a whole new world out there to explore. A new dimension. And within no time at all, you'll have become so consumed by your new passion in life that the past will seem trivial by comparison. You'll have purpose and direction and others will begin, once again, to look to you for guidance. You'll be regarded by those around you as a pillar of the community; the one person able to exert real influence when it is needed. You will have taken up knitting. You will. That's what all FYOs do, didn't you know? And there is just so much work to get through: booties, mittens, woolly hats, cardies; life will simply never be the same again. No, you will never need to look back, you will have found your true vocation in life.

Don't you just wish it could have happened twenty-years ago?, — all that wasted time! It's enough to make you want to top yourself, eh? No, if it's all the same to you, I'll pass on this one. FYOdom is for other people, not me. I'm really not cut out for it. Never was. Life as a sub-FYO suits me fine — you know what they say: if it ain't broke don't fix it . . . hold on a minute, must get the phone, excuse me . . . "Hello pet, how are things? I beg your pardon? Say that again. You're what? Are you sure? When did you, I mean, er, when is it, er, oh my God . . ."